somabasics

garden design

somabasics
garden design

David Stevens

SOMA

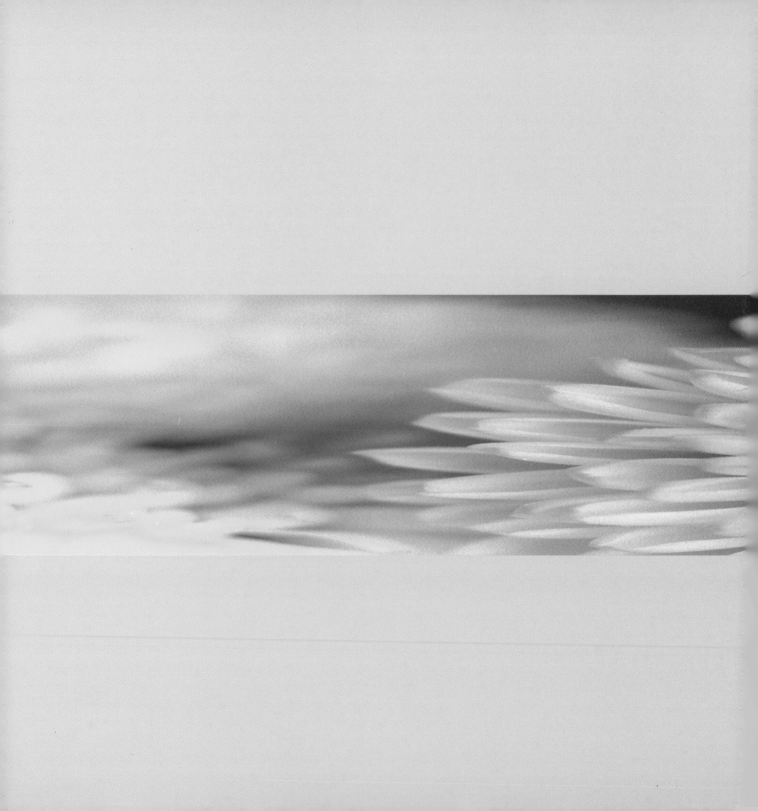

contents

introduction

Good design has nothing to do with fashion.

The whole subject of garden design has become increasingly popular over the past few years, and it has generated a plethora of television shows, books and magazines. While this is both exciting and positive, much of the material has been lightweight, with many self-styled experts being concerned with immediate effect rather than lasting appeal. Gardens and garden design are not about a "quick fix"; they are a wonderful mixture of horticulture, art and architecture, and they offer us the opportunity to create a personal space that fits us like a glove. Every composition will be different because each of us has different characteristics and needs. When you think about it, hardly anything in this world, whether a car or a suit of clothes, is designed specifically for us, and perhaps the most rewarding aspect of owning a garden is the simple fact that this is *our* space, to do with what we will. In all probability, this will be the largest space over which we have complete control—a prospect that is immensely attractive, and also slightly daunting.

Right *House and garden are inseparable elements, and in the best compositions there is a seamless link between inside and out. The modern and minimalist movements stripped away the old architectural preconceptions, allowing us the freedom to look at our living environment in an entirely different way.*

While most of us can make a pretty good attempt at organizing the spaces, colors and ornamentation of our homes, much of this good sense dries up when we move outside. This is partly due to the fact that we are encouraged to think of gardening and design as difficult subjects, which in fact they are not. The design of gardens, like anything else, should be essentially simple, reflecting both our lifestyle and our immediate surroundings.

One of the problems is that we are overwhelmed with choices: there are garden centers around every corner, each one stuffed with horticultural goodies. This encourages the fatal habit of impulse buying, without thought for the size and requirement of the plants. Add to this a wealth of sundries, including arbors, arches, pools, statues, pots and paving, and it's no small wonder that many a garden ends up as a mass of unrelated features. Design, on the other hand, encourages control; it allows you to plan the spaces and components in a way that suits you and your family. Good design has nothing to do with fashion, which is a transient thing, and everything to do with a tried and tested set of rules that will work under virtually any circumstances. These are the designer's tools and tricks of the trade; there is nothing mysterious or difficult about them, and at the end of the day they come down to sound common sense.

My trade for the past thirty years has been that of creating gardens, thousands of them—no two have ever been the same. Over that time I have evolved a sequence of planning that is simple and straightforward.

Your garden is a uniquely valuable place, and this book takes you through each step of planning it effectively. We start with getting to know the site and move on to planning the various elements, demystifying the planting process and creating the design. Finally, we see how several real gardens were created from less-than-promising spaces. Above everything, gardens and gardening should be fun, giving you somewhere to relax, dine, entertain, play and simply escape from the everyday pressures of life.

Above *The best gardens have a relaxed and easygoing attitude that owes nothing to fashion but everything to the owner. Personality above all else drives this garden, making it unique. Its key components are foliage and understated color, in a low-maintenance design that fits the owner like a glove.*

groundwork

Before tackling any job, you must take stock, get a feel of the area and have a good look at the surroundings. You will also want to think about a style that appeals in both practical and aesthetic terms, providing a visual link between the house and garden to create a single, seamless composition.

getting to know your garden

Gardens are intimate places, which become all the more intimate as you get to know them better. Yours may be a brand-new garden with nothing but stark boundaries, or it may be well established with a wealth of interesting features and mature planting. There may have been something about the garden, or the way that the house sits within it, that drew you into moving there in the first place. First impressions can be very useful, but it will pay dividends if you can wait a while before actually embarking on the design. During your first year you may see spring bulbs pushing their way to the surface, first the snowdrops and crocuses and then the daffodils and tulips. Next come herbaceous plants, hardy perennials and summer-flowering shrubs. Autumn brings a blaze of foliage, while the crisp outlines of trees and other structure plants provide winter interest. When you come to work out a planting scheme, these existing plants can often provide the bones of a plan.

Your first year can be quietly spent in maintaining the garden and getting to know its various moods, all of which will influence your thinking and the design that emerges from it.

The height of the sun and the length of the shadows it casts will vary from winter to summer. In summer the sun will be high in the sky and the amount of shade in your garden will be reduced as a result. This will have obvious implications for the positioning of a sunny sitting area or a shady seat. The way that the sun swings throughout the day will also determine your choice of plants and the locations of ponds, vegetable patches and other features. Bear in mind that in small gardens, seasonal variations in the positioning of sunny and shady areas can have much more impact than in larger gardens.

You must also remember that a garden can never exist in isolation. It will be contained by a larger environment that has a distinct character of its own. The choice of materials for boundaries or paving should be directed by your immediate surroundings. Regional variations in soil and climate will determine the species of plant that thrive on your plot. It is always sensible to respect local conditions. Of course, you can import materials from wherever you like, but they will seldom look comfortable and will probably cost a small fortune in transportation expenses.

Above *Your decision about where to position a sitting area will depend on a number of considerations, including the available sun or shade, and proximity to the house. This deck blends beautifully with the surrounding trees and shrubs, creating a self-contained space that gives a feeling of peacefulness and seclusion.*

Above *Borrowed landscape allows a glimpse of your neighbor's garden or a view out to the countryside. Make the most of it, perhaps with a focus of carefully positioned trees.*

Above *The effect here might seem ever so slightly contrived, with the ogee window picking up the shape of the garden gazebo. That aside, there is a wonderful feeling of moving between interior and exterior living space, the door offering an open invitation to explore the great outdoors.*

Drawing neighboring property or countryside into your garden in this way will increase the feeling of space in your own area, and add a sense of adventure in the act of peering through.

Your first year can be quietly spent in maintaining the garden and getting to know its various moods, all of which will influence your thinking and the design that emerges from it.

Opposite *Green foliage sets off the crisp lines of a modern house to perfection, introducing a natural note without detracting from the architecture.*

basic surveying

By simply looking after your garden during this first year you will really start to get inside the character of the place. You can use the time to carry out a survey that will form the basis of a scale drawing and the design to follow. This is both simple and enjoyable. It will mean identifying every aspect of your house and garden.

To make a survey drawing you need a 100-foot tape measure, notepad, pencil and clipboard. First sketch the outline of the house and its boundaries before taking what are known as "running measurements" of the length and width of the garden. Start by fixing the tape to the fence or boundary on one side and unreel it across the face of the building, toward the opposite boundary, leaving it on the ground. Write down the measurements in sequence, starting with the edge of the house and including the positions of doors, windows, drains, manholes and other important features. Then do the same down the length of the garden, noting existing trees, shrubs, buildings, paths and all other features. Mark everything on your scale drawing, because the most unlikely things—an old hedge partway across the garden or a large conifer that at first appears to have no appeal whatsoever—could end up being the pivot of a new design. Don't remove anything until you are absolutely certain—it takes five minutes to fell a tree, but many years to grow one.

If your garden has a boundary set at an angle, or you want to plot the position of a feature some way from the fence line, you can use a simple technique called triangulation. Run a tape from a known point, say one corner of the building, to the feature in question and note the measurement. Now move the tape to another known point and repeat the operation. When you transfer the measurements onto a scale drawing, you can use a pair of compasses to draw two arcs with radii of the measurements you noted. Where these intersect will be the exact position of the feature.

Make a note of changes of level, slopes, and good or—more importantly—bad views. Note prevailing winds and particularly cold or drafty corners as well as areas of sun and shade. Mark the exact position of north on your plan, using a compass if necessary. Check the soil type with the kind of simple kit that is readily available at garden centers. Some gardens may have additional problems such as traffic noise or pollution, so make a note of these on your scale drawing too, since these may have an effect on how you lay out the space.

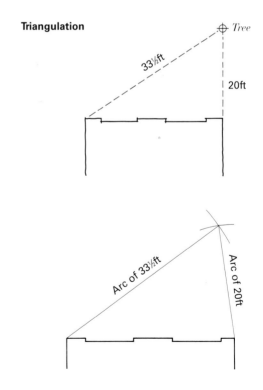

Triangulation

$Tree$

$33\frac{1}{2}$ft

20ft

Arc of $33\frac{1}{2}$ft

Arc of 20ft

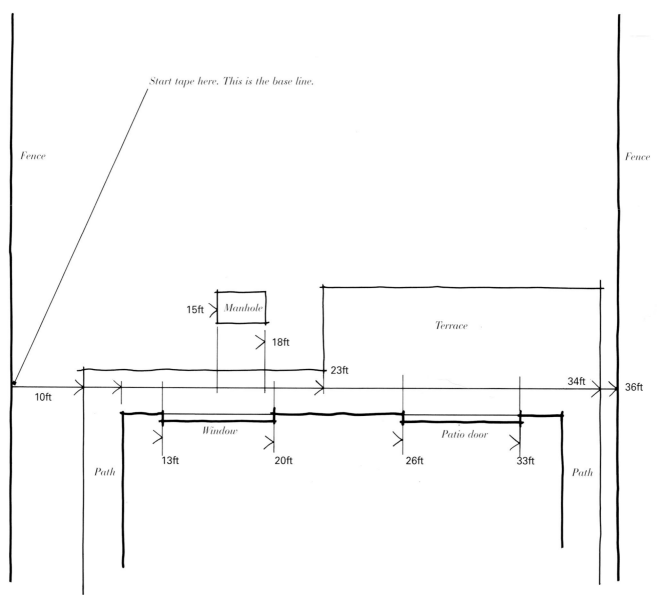

Start tape here. This is the base line.

Fence

Fence

15ft

Manhole

18ft

Terrace

23ft

10ft

34ft

36ft

Window

13ft

20ft

Patio door

26ft

33ft

Path

Path

Above *A survey drawing detailing the positions of features within a garden. It is not drawn to scale—a survey drawing is a freehand sketch of the house and garden, to which "running measurements" are added.*
Left *Triangulation can be used to plot the exact position of certain features.*

choosing a style

Just as no two people are alike, neither are their gardens. A garden cannot simply be copied from a book, television program or garden show, since the designs you find there will have been created from a totally different set of criteria. You will want to gather information from all these sources when you are starting out; you may also want to visit or revisit gardens that are open to the public to remind you of the types of gardens you have particularly liked or disliked in the past. Remember, though, that it will be impossible, as well as undesirable, to reproduce exactly what you have seen elsewhere. You can certainly gain isolated ideas from shows, books and public gardens and they will be a source of inspiration, but that is all.

The first step in deciding on a style for your garden should always be to look at the interior of your house. The kind of living space that you have created inside the house will provide a pretty accurate clue about the kind of garden you will be comfortable with. Are you a modernist, with a liking for upbeat materials and design, or a traditionalist, feeling more comfortable with period furniture, patterns and fabrics? Be perfectly honest with yourself and don't be seduced by the media, or by the opinions of garden gurus.

Opposite *This formal design is modern and understated, and complements perfectly the style of the house to which it is attached. Decking—reflecting the construction materials of the house—is punctuated by symmetrically placed pots of daisies and edged by clipped boxwood hedging, leading the eye to the steps in the distance.*

preparing a mood board

One of the best ways of building an image of just what you want is by preparing a "mood board." Collect pictures of complete gardens, individual areas, pools, paving, focal points and plants, and pin them up on a big board. Add images as the months pass, and share the process with the whole family. As well as photographs or ads showing specific features, include color charts, swatches of fabric, samples of gravel and anything else that you feel may have potential or you find particularly appealing. This activity will help you refine your concept of just what you want, allowing you to home in on a specific garden style.

looking at the garden in context

Many people have a tendency to think of their garden as an isolated space. This is a real problem in design terms. The simple fact is that the garden cannot be separated from the house, on the one hand, or the areas *outside* its boundaries, on the other. The house will often suggest the style of the garden and the materials used in it. A period house, built perhaps in brick, might well suggest the creation of a paved area constructed from brick and a hard surfacing material laid together in a formal pattern. This would provide the frame for a balanced design. A modern building, on the other hand, could be the cue for crisp, geometric shapes that reflect the façade and continue out into the garden in an asymmetrical pattern. In other words, the inspiration for the garden's design and the materials used in it must come from the house and the immediate location.

While the space within the boundaries is obviously of prime importance, remember the potential for using "borrowed landscape." If your neighbor has a fine group of shrubs, screen your boundary with planting to make some of the species next door appear to be part of your own space. If there is no sharp division between the gardens and the planting groups appear to merge together, both gardens will feel larger. In an area with more open space, a fine view can be framed with planting. You can incorporate a see-through post-and-rail or metal fence into the view, thus drawing the vista toward you and making your garden feel much larger.

Opposite Minimalism expressed in the most elegant of ways— these low, clipped hedges perfectly unify building and landscape. Maintenance is also minimal. It's a beautiful example of good design.
Right *Linkage here is at an altogether higher level, way above the street in a roof garden. The white overhead trellises float over the garden, extending the line of the building outward.*

Above *The junction between house and garden is barely perceptible, with planting linking the vertical and horizontal planes in a sweep of flower and foliage.*

different styles
within the garden

Whatever the geographic location of your garden, there are really only three basic design styles from which to choose: formal, asymmetrical and free-form. We will look at these options in detail a little later on (see pages 34–35). Don't worry at this stage about such things as cottage, Japanese or Italianate styles; these are simply the names of gardens from particular countries or cultures. You can in fact have a formal or informal cottage garden, just as you can have a formal or informal Japanese-style garden.

Whichever style you choose, the impact of your garden depends on the use of space within it and your ability to create a strong architectural link with the house. The link should be forged by the progression of space and the use of compatible shapes and building materials. As you move away from the house the design can become softer, looser and less formal. In other words, close to the house you may well think of using crisp, overlapping rectangles of paving, softened by planting. This area could give way to flowing curves occupying the middle distance, while the furthest part of the garden could drift into informal planting. Much of this effect can be achieved through the underlying "hard landscape" or design structure, and the planting that overlays it. The planting scheme can be designed to enhance the existing structure.

The overall climatic conditions and the microclimate of the particular area should also be reflected in the selection of plants. For example, Mediterranean species should be placed in the real hot spots of the garden and woodland plants should go in those cool, dark places. In other words, with a modicum of homework you should always be able to get the right plant in the right place.

Whichever style you choose, the impact of your garden depends on your use of space and your ability to create a strong architectural link with the house.

Left *Modern minimalism can be strikingly beautiful, with regularly spaced planting that is architectural in its own right, linking the repetitive elements in the building. The ground cover of stones introduces a wonderful earthy look.*

planning

the elements

By now you will have developed a real feel for your garden—you know its ins and outs, its advantages and disadvantages, and its many idiosyncrasies. You will have assembled a mood board and checked out just what your family members want and need. Beyond this you will have also become aware of the wider garden setting, the landscape or townscape, and how this may influence your proposals.

your space

Below *The division of space is central to many forms of design and to garden design in particular, serving to increase the impression of overall space as you move through a composition. Where a view is framed by a door, window or other opening, there is an inevitable feeling of mystery about what lies beyond. Tension increases as you approach and there finally comes a surprise as the new view opens into a new garden "room."*

A garden that feels right and comfortable is one that truly reflects its owner's needs, but how do we go about making our own dreams a reality? In truth, you are probably a good deal closer than you think, since many ideas will have started to formulate during the initial fact-finding period. Unlike a professional designer, you have had time on your side. However good a designer might be, he or she can never achieve your intimate understanding of your garden or your family's needs.

dividing space

The design of gardens has much to do with the manipulation and division of space. Pattern, color, texture and other, more subtle, factors are also important, but it will be the division of space that determines the way in which the garden works. Think of an empty room or a bare garden: both room and garden become far more interesting as soon as you start dividing the space, breaking the sight lines with screens of some kind. In a garden these can include walls, trellises, hedges and plants. In a large garden there could be many such divisions, but even in the smallest city yard a simple trellis or carefully positioned plant can be enough to interrupt the view and introduce interest.

circles

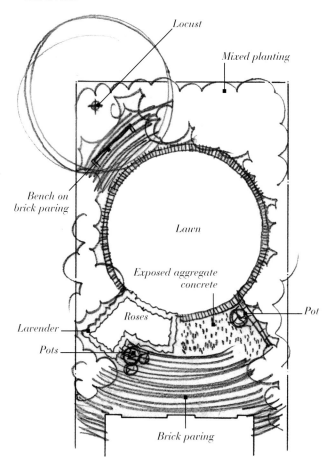

Locust

Mixed planting

Bench on brick paving

Lawn

Exposed aggregate concrete

Roses

Pot

Lavender

Pots

Brick paving

Above *A circular pattern inevitably leads the eye away from rectangular boundaries, turning in on itself to create interest within the space. Everything here is based on a single, central radius, and materials used include brick, gravel, turf and planting. Although this is only a sketch, it is practically a finished design and would, like the other drawings shown here, work perfectly with just a little tidying up.*

controlled informality

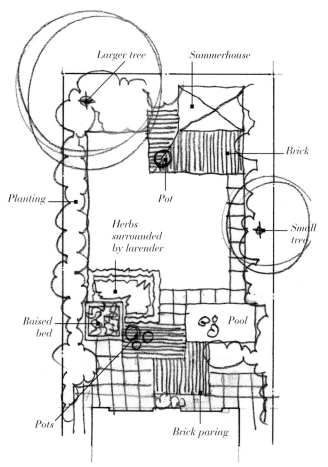

Larger tree

Summerhouse

Brick

Planting

Pot

Small tree

Herbs surrounded by lavender

Raised bed

Pool

Pots

Brick paving

Above *This is an asymmetrical design where one part of the garden balances another—in this case the visual weight of the terrace is offset by the summerhouse and sitting area in the upper right-hand corner. There are no curved lines at all, a style that is anathema to some garden owners and designers, but when planted this kind of composition looks both controlled and elegant.*

deconstructivist

curves and diagonals

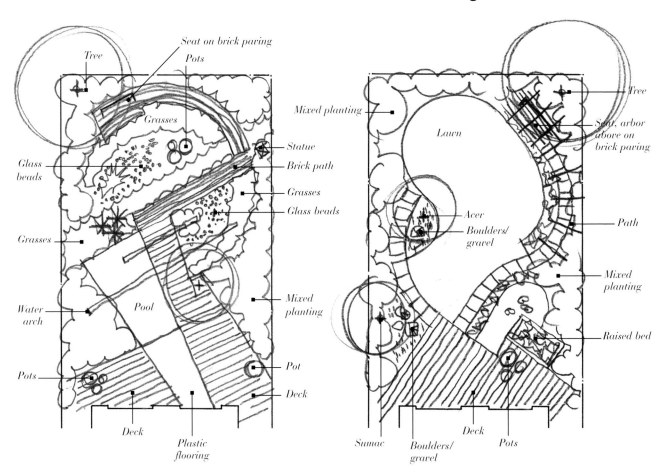

deconstructivist diagram labels:
Seat on brick paving
Tree
Pots
Grasses
Statue
Glass beads
Brick path
Grasses
Glass beads
Grasses
Mixed planting
Water arch
Pool
Pots
Pot
Deck
Deck
Plastic flooring

curves and diagonals diagram labels:
Mixed planting
Lawn
Tree
Seat, arbor above on brick paving
Acer
Boulders/gravel
Path
Mixed planting
Raised bed
Deck
Sumac
Boulders/gravel
Pots

Above *Not many designers are into this kind of work, but I certainly am. Such a style breaks, or at least stretches, the conventional design rules to the limit, and often aggressively uses contrasting shapes and angles to overlap or interpenetrate one another. Here the decking and pool set up a carefully contrived dialogue with the curving brick path and grasses. Blue glass beads act as a lightly reflective lawn or ground cover.*

Above *A diagonal is the longest available line within a rectangle, and designers often use them as a trick of the trade for increasing the feeling of space within a garden. The deck or paving is placed diagonally at 45 degrees, and paths sweep away in two directions, giving access to the lawn and seat. The latter is spanned by an arbor, which continues above the path on its way to the house. Lawn and border shapes are built up from strong radiused curves.*

formal

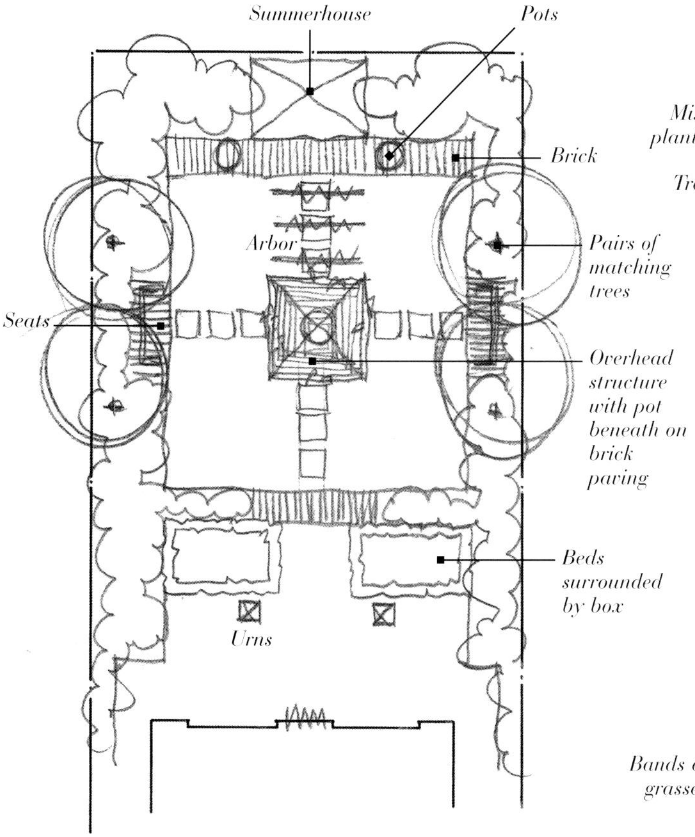

Summerhouse

Pots

Brick

Arbor

Pairs of matching trees

Seats

Overhead structure with pot beneath on brick paving

Beds surrounded by box

Urns

free-form

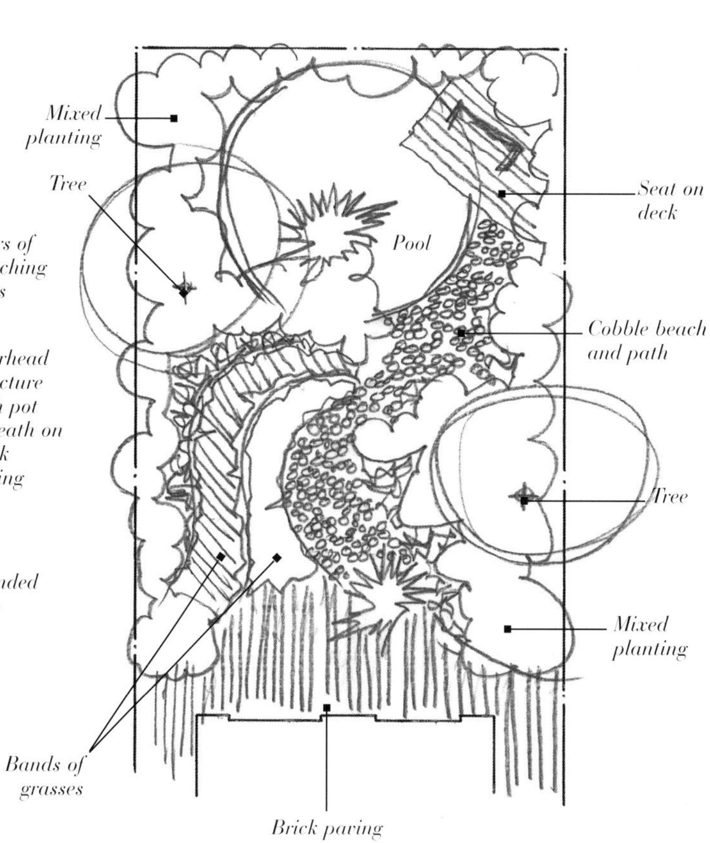

Mixed planting

Tree

Pool

Seat on deck

Cobble beach and path

Tree

Mixed planting

Bands of grasses

Brick paving

Above *Formal designs rely on balance, and a mirror image from side to side or end to end. In this garden there are two axes: the more dominant leads away from the house, passes under the central gazebo and terminates at the summerhouse flanked by pots. A secondary axis is set at right angles leading across the lawn, focusing on the two seats framed by matching pairs of trees.*

Above *This style of garden is the most difficult to get right, requiring an instinctive feeling for balance and proportion. Informality must be balanced against providing a visual link with the house. Brick paving or decking gives way to a cobble path and beach flanking a circular pool. A seat faces the pool, again on a diagonal, while planting both reinforces the curve of the beach and softens the boundaries.*

garden styles

I have already mentioned the three basic garden styles: formal, asymmetrical and free-form, all of which can use subdivision as part of the overall design. In formal gardens, which can be of any size, one side will mirror the other. Precise geometry is the key, together with immaculate detailing. Parterres of clipped hedging, carefully positioned ornaments, regularly patterned lawns and calm pools can all be part of a formal garden. These are controlled spaces, intended to slow the visitor down and give a feeling of permanence and stability; they are not usually suited to rambunctious play.

Asymmetrical gardens also depend on balance and geometry, but in a very different way. Imagine a fulcrum that has been brought into perfect equilibrium by a heavy weight close to the balance point and a lighter weight further away from it. In a garden you can balance the visual weight of a terrace or paved area to one side of the design with a major focal point, perhaps a rock feature or a building, situated slightly further away on the other side. Similar "balancing acts" can be achieved with tree groups, water features or patterns of paving, planting and raised beds on a terrace. Asymmetry is the medium of modernism. These designs look best around buildings of irregular outline rather than those with formal façades.

Opposite left *Glimpses are so attractive, beckoning you on to a new garden room, which in this case has a centrally positioned bowl around which the design revolves. The distant view is blocked by hedges, but what lies beyond?*

Opposite right *Classic linkage and a beautifully simple asymmetrical composition. Some may find it too controlled, but it suits the owner's tastes and it would suit me just fine too.*

Free-form or "organic" gardens are just what they sound like. While the formal and asymmetrical styles depend on strict geometry, this one does not. Shapes are soft and fluid, reflecting those seen in a lowland landscape or meandering river. They are never contorted or contrived. This style is not always an easy option, and sensitivity is needed in order for the design to succeed. When done well, however, a free-form approach can produce a wonderfully relaxed and informal garden.

Style has nothing to do with a particular period of history. It is perfectly possible to create a high-tech or cottage garden that is either formal or informal. The key is simply to link them with the building by using compatible materials.

small spaces

The smaller a space the more difficult it will be to sub-divide (although it may well be possible to incorporate a secret corner). In a tiny garden you should try to maximize the area. Doors that can be opened wide work to unite interior and exterior space. Soften boundaries with planting, and, if one boundary is particularly dominant, *never* draw attention to it with a focal point. Position an eye-catcher to one side in order to draw the eye away to another part of the garden. In such places try using mirrors, false doors and perspectives, murals and trompe l'oeil. Avoid bright colors, which demand attention, and go instead for cool tones and pastel shades, which tend to make a space feel larger.

Above *In a tiny rectangular roof garden a circular pattern has been introduced to provide movement and interest. Decking is light and practical, an important consideration for a roof garden, and the chairs are definitely inviting.*

structure

If we are going to divide our garden into separate areas we need to decide how these divisions will be made. In part this will be an aesthetic choice, but cost will also play an important role since some materials are far more expensive than others.

boundaries & dividers

Your main boundaries, be they walls, fences or hedges, will probably already be in position, and as it is often prohibitively expensive and impractical to remove them, it is usually best to leave them in position and allow them to provide the cue for any divisions within the garden. Boundaries often have the visual effect of extending the line of an adjoining building into the garden. Brick or stone houses look superb with boundary walls of similar materials. These are the most expensive and the most durable options. Timber fences are cheaper and can link in well with timber trellises or dividers within the garden. Hedges are cheapest of all, but they require regular clipping and feeding. If the view out of the garden is attractive—for instance in a rural location—a "see-through" boundary in the form of a post-and-rail fence may be ideal (although it may offer little in the way of security).

Opposite *Gates and openings are immensely inviting, particularly when set within a solid wall. The concrete steps are beautifully detailed in cast concrete, similar to the wall, while planting stands out in sharp relief, acting as a frame and focus to the door.*
Below *Walls provide an outer line of defense, or at least shelter and definition, in a modern garden. This wonderfully fluid line naturally leads the eye toward the church tower—an excellent example of borrowed landscape.*

paved areas

Together with boundaries, the paved areas of the garden will take the lion's share of your budget, so careful planning is essential. The paving can create another strong visual link with the house. Old rectangular stone paving is the most costly material, but the simulated version can look almost as good at a fraction of the cost. In a contemporary setting, precast concrete slabs are an excellent choice for a terrace, perhaps teamed with brick. Decking and exposed aggregate concrete are also popular. Steps can be built from any of these materials. They should be as broad and generous as possible.

Smooth surfaces are ideal beneath tables and chairs, but uneven finishes, such as cobblestone and granite, give texture and grip, making them useful for paths and drives. Gravel, laid correctly on a binder, is also ideal and can be used for large, informal areas, where plants can be allowed to grow through its surface.

soft surfaces

In many gardens the soft surfaces of lawn and planting occupy the greatest area. Of these, lawns will take the largest share, providing a calm backdrop and tying the composition together. In a formal design the lawn will be crisp and rectangular, perhaps framed by screens or hedges, while in an informal garden the shapes will be altogether more fluid. Always keep the outlines as simple as possible so that they are easy to mow and maintain. Remember not to take a lawn too close to a boundary, because this will leave you with a very narrow border. Ensure that entrances are sufficiently wide to prevent undue wear, or incorporate a paved apron, perhaps spanned by an arch or arbor.

Large areas can be planted with ground-cover plants in island beds or deep borders that will merge together in wonderful drifts.

Opposite above *There should always be a balance between hard and soft surfaces, and this grass grid is the perfect foil to the glass block paving.*

Opposite below *The combination of galvanized fencing and trellis is an unusual but effective one. Low-key planting and clipped trees offer an ideal counterpoint.*

Above *A study in impeccable detail much in the style of Sir Edwin Lutyens. Tiles set on edge combine well with brick and concrete paving.*

Above right *There is a logical extension of pattern from the planting to paving that sets up its own rhythm.*

Right *In this relatively soft planting design a degree of control is introduced by the brown stepping stones, which provide both access and a strong directional emphasis.*

paths & routes

In any garden you will need to get around the place, whether it is a backyard or a country estate. In some situations it will simply be a matter of getting from A to B as quickly as possible, something that is called a "desire line." This is the most obvious and straight-forward use of paths in the garden, but not the only one. Paths can also be used as a positive design tool to create a feeling of space, making the garden feel larger. If you are subdividing an area, why not take a path up one side of the garden, across, and up the other side. You could create a zigzag path to reinforce a diagonal pattern, or a curved one to echo circular design elements. In a fluid design a path can flow around the garden, from room to room, leading the feet past borders or other garden features.

The way in which you lay paving can also be a useful, but easily overlooked, design tool. Slabs or bricks in a staggered bond laid *away* from you, or down a path, accelerate the view, tending to foreshorten it. The path will appear to be shorter than it actually is. These same materials laid *across* a path or vista, however, positively slow the eye down, increasing the feeling of space and making the journey appear longer.

Opposite left *Steps and changes of level should be both elegant and practical. These steps are comfortable and their horizontal lines are offset by the tall mulleins.*

Opposite right *An unusual material—metal washers—is separated by a single black step. The harshness of the man-made material is offset by the planting softening the line of the path.*

Above left *This stone path has a naturally "country" feel, associating well with a cottage style of planting. Being slightly*

uneven, the path slows you down, which allows you to enjoy the space as you move through it. Ideally it should be built from the same stone as boundary walls and the adjoining house.

Above right *The bridge, hand rails and grass path all combine to accelerate the view. Your eye quite literally rushes down the space, drawing you briskly onward. The power of a view can be enormous, so use it with understanding.*

views & focal points

I have already touched on the subject of borrowed landscape (see page 24), which can be particularly valuable in increasing the visual size of your garden. Remember that for this technique to work at its best you need to disguise your boundary and then plant species in your garden to link with those visible in your neighbor's plot. A similar technique can be used in a country garden where there may be a fine landscape outlook. In this case it can be most effective to frame the view to either side with planting that will provide a focus and draw the view back into your own garden. Bad views can naturally be blotted out with all kinds of devices, including planting, hedges, trellises and screens. Don't forget that a bad or intrusive view can also be *above* your eye line, one example being a neighbor's window overlooking your garden. In this case, a carefully positioned tree could be the answer. Alternatively, you might be able to screen the garden sitting area with overhead beams that run out from the house or boundary. An arbor can perform much the same function, and if clothed with climbers can be an attractive feature in itself. If a bad view is particularly dominant and difficult to screen, the best approach may be to establish a powerful focal point in another part of the garden so that it will positively draw the eye away from the problem area.

planting

Planting brings the garden alive, providing color and interest throughout the year and softening the underlying hard landscape structure. Plants can also divide your space, provide screens and reinforce the shapes of borders, leading the eye in a particular sequence through the garden. The planting design may be architectural or relaxed—its style will reflect your personality and the amount of maintenance you are prepared to undertake. Remember that a minimalist grouping of accent plants requires little work, but it looks good in the right setting.

placing plants

Most people find themselves impulse buying at the garden center, or they are the lucky recipients of plants and cuttings from friends or relatives. Consequently, plants often end up being placed at random, with no real thought given to their needs or eventual size. The first and most obvious rule is *read the label*. This really will help you to plant them in the right place. Planting is not difficult if you approach it logically. The secret is to follow the layered approach. The outer envelope and the background planting should be tough and largely evergreen to provide shelter and screening. In the middle of the borders the medium-sized shrubs and taller hardy perennials hold sway, while at the front, at the lowest level of all, you can use the ground cover to form a carpet and reduce maintenance. In all the layers try to plant in drifts and groups to give your design more continuity. You will also reduce the need for weeding by covering the ground between plants more effectively when you plant in groups.

Opposite *There is a delicious softness and verticality associated with many grasses, which here is relieved by the textural line of Jerusalem sage.* **Right** *A casual seat and a background of relaxed planting, some in containers and some permanent. Such an approach, although seemingly haphazard, is nevertheless carefully planned.*

using color

There are many different theories about using color in the garden, but ultimately success revolves around understanding the difference between hot and cool ranges. Bright colors, like red, orange and yellow, are vibrant and they draw the eye. If placed at the bottom of the garden they demand attention and foreshorten the space. Keep them close to the house or main viewpoint and let the pastel colors drift into the distance. Gray foliage is a great harmonizer, toning down and tying color ranges together, while white can be used to create sharp highlights in either range.

growing food

While a fully planted vegetable garden takes a deal of time to tend, there are many vegetables, fruits and herbs that can be grown with minimal fuss, either in a specific plot, or mixed with the borders. Many vegetables are

Above *Some compositions are simply wacky, but why not? This is a gloriously eclectic collection of containers, plants and artifacts that creates a very personal space.*
Right *The color linkage here is crafty and heightened by the sharp flower of flannel bush.*

exceedingly handsome—you could hardly have a more productive or good-looking annual climber than runner beans—so think positive and don't hide them away. A grouping of bamboo canes covered in healthy runner bean plants not only produces fresh food but is also an interesting vertical design element in a border.

instant effects

Pots and containers are marvelous for providing instant color, particularly when used close to the house on a terrace or paved area. When the flowers fade, the pots can then be moved to a less prominent position. As a general rule, keep things simple when selecting and grouping pots, choosing a theme of terra cotta, stone or timber containers, for example, and remember, the bigger the pot the happier the plants will be, particularly if they are fed and watered regularly.

Above *Who said that the only function of hanging baskets was decoration? Here is an unusual but practical planting that is not unattractive.*
Left *Sun-bleached timber and mirrors make this composition feel much larger than it really is. It has a slightly quirky feel due to the distorted images of plants, and it proves that there is always room for lateral thinking in garden design.*

living areas

If we think of our garden as an outside room, we can see that it is logical to apply some of the principles used in interior design to the space outside. In the same way as the house contains different areas for different activities, so the garden can be broken down into zones which fulfill different functions. There will be quiet places for relaxation and lively ones used for play. There will also be utility areas, since every garden has to contain practical as well as aesthetic elements.

seating areas

It usually makes sense to position the main seating area close to the house, opening out from the interior living spaces. Not only are you more likely to use the space if it is easily accessible, it is also easier and more practical, when you are entertaining guests for example, to ferry food and drinks to and from the house. In temperate climates an open, sunny place is ideal. If the rear of the house is in shade for much of the day, the seating area may need to be placed further away in order to catch the sun. In hot climates the reverse applies. This is where verandas are so useful, not only enabling you to eat outside even in the heat of the midday sun, but also providing a wonderfully shady link with the building.

You should also consider the time of the day you are most likely to be using your seating area—if you are unlikely to be sitting out during the day, it makes sense to choose an area that catches the evening, rather than the morning, sun.

Construction materials will look most comfortable if they reflect those used in the house, especially when used in the right combination. I always feel that an area with surfaces made from a single material, say brick, is visually a little too "heavy." Three materials used together can appear "busy," while two can be just right, providing both contrast and balance. Also, seating areas close to the house should be architectural in character, but those farther away can be less formal, having an irregular outline of bricks, sets, wood blocks or broken paving that blends into an informal setting.

Opposite *Some spaces simply work well. There is an enormous feeling of tranquility in this Japanese-influenced design. Like all good work it is mercifully simple, with a sparing use of materials, resulting in a fine and practical living area.*

children's areas

Having been through the family experience, I have come to realize that children will always play where they please, no matter how many carefully thought out play areas you have included in your garden design. The best places are often created spontaneously, and they are liable to change. At times children might be attracted to a hidden den in the shrubbery, at others they are drawn to sliding on trays down slopes or digging pools in some out-of-the-way and horrendously muddy area. Much play equipment looks awful, but the stoutest and most expensive kind is often the best, from the point of view of both safety and durability. To avoid injury, swings need plenty of room around them and chipped bark or grass underneath them.

Children rarely want to garden formally, and plots set aside for children's use are usually quickly forgotten. Far better to let them plant spectacular and fast-growing things in the general borders. Sunflowers and nasturtiums are always favorites with children, and they have the added advantage that their large seeds are easy for small fingers to handle.

Right Children want, and should have, fun—it's what growing up is all about! This elegant play place is in quite a different league from the usual plastic play houses. Sound construction is essential for a structure like this, and this one even has a roof for all-weather play.

garden structures

Garden structures act as major focal points, drawing the eye and demanding attention. As such they need to be carefully positioned so that they are in harmony with the overall garden design. Features such as gazebos are static and look best tucked into the planting. Arches and arbors encourage movement. They should always lead you in a positive direction, such as to another part of the garden, or to a minor focal point—never the shed, compost bin or incinerator!

Above right *Timber is a natural material for use in gardens, blending well into most situations. As a rule, substantial structures look best, and these can either be stained or painted to pick up a color elsewhere in the garden. This wooden structure sits well between complementary wings of planting.*

Right *Delicate traceries, particularly in iron and of ample size, can be very effective as they allow the viewer to focus on the planting rather than the structure itself. The lines of this archway, with its solid brick piers, lead the eye down the path to the classical urn.*

services

Right *Water is the provider of life in a garden, and rain, gathered in a barrel, can be a useful source.*
Below *Storage, and plenty of it, is essential. Never underestimate how much you might need, and always provide a sound work table as well as shelves.*
Bottom *With an imaginative paint scheme, a shed can be transformed into a fashion accessory.*

Services, which are an essential element of an attractive garden, should be concealed within it. Water, in addition to serving the practical function of keeping plants alive, can serve a decorative function in pools and fountains. One or more taps will be invaluable. Frostproof them in colder climates. They can be the pick-up points for hoses or simple irrigation systems. More sophisticated systems can be plumbed in directly from the house.

Electricity is another essential, driving everything from submersible pumps and lights to growing systems in the greenhouse. If in doubt with *anything* electrical, enlist a professional—better safe than sorry. Lighting can be both functional and decorative, and sometimes both. Steps, garages, doorways, paths and sitting areas may well need illumination, and there are some marvellous techniques to highlight specific garden areas. With lighting, less is more. And stick to blue or white light—other colors can make foliage look very unattractive.

In many gardens, you can plan an integrated work space for shed, greenhouse, compost and incinerator, with ample standing room and easy access, all of which can be neatly screened. If you have large or boisterous dogs, they may need their own run and, as a final thought, you may want to include a clothes line.

Right *Lighting can be moody, bright, decorative or utilitarian. With imagination, it can be all of these things, as in this scheme which incorporated both uplights and downlights. In a garden or outside living space, pools of light are far more effective than blanket coverage, so think carefully before implementing a scheme.*

creating

the design

Up to this point you have been gathering information, but now it is time to start making your ideas come alive. There are many ways to do this, including making rough sketches, marking out shapes in the garden, and even using movable sections of trellis or fencing to create different "rooms."

Below *This garden is both uncompromising and offers a clean slate, so any design can start from scratch.*
Right *A classic treatment that maximizes space is to lead a path—constructed in this proposal from brick paving and precast concrete slabs—from the patio, up and across the garden, and up the garden to the seat at the back. This creates distinct garden "rooms" as well as diverting the feet from the direct "desire line." This in turn helps to create a feeling of greater space. The path terminates at a seat while the shed is neatly screened by trellis.*

Tree

Wing of planting

Seat and screen to shed

Tree

Path

Raised bed

Lawn

Patio

concept drawings

The important thing at this stage is not to crystallize your plans too soon. After all, you have probably spent a year collecting information, so another week or two will not make the slightest difference.

Bringing your ideas to life is exciting, and one of the best tricks of the trade used by professional designers is creating visualization overlays. This simply involves

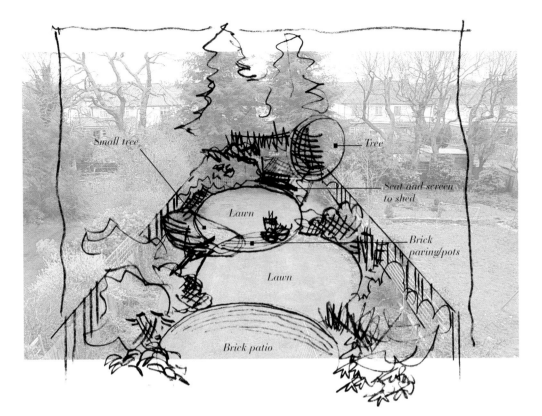

Small tree

Tree

Seat and screen
to shed

Lawn

Brick
paving/pots

Lawn

Brick patio

Left *With this treatment,
overlapping circles
provide a real feeling
of movement, positively
distracting from those
rectangular boundaries
and turning the design
in upon itself. Brick
overlaps provide pause
points, the central one
hosting a group of
posts. The seat again
fits neatly at the top
while planting softens
and surrounds the
composition. In both
gardens the conifers
provide screening as
well as a positively
sculptural outline.*

laying tracing paper over a photograph of your garden, on to which can be sketched various ideas. This will allow you to work out sight lines, lines of desire and focal points, as well as positions of trees, planting and furniture. Take a photograph of the garden from an upstairs window, if possible, allowing you to see as much of the existing layout as possible, and offering a realistic sense of perspective. If you want to add items such as garden buildings or other structures to your drawing, you can trace them directly from a magazine or catalog. Try as many different ideas as you like, take your time and don't just settle on the first design you draw. Paper is cheap, so have fun working out all the permutations.

Multistemmed tree
to screen window

Gazebo

Top
lawn

Path

Near lawn

Herb
bed

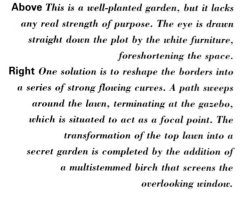

Above *This is a well-planted garden, but it lacks
any real strength of purpose. The eye is drawn
straight down the plot by the white furniture,
foreshortening the space.*
Right *One solution is to reshape the borders into
a series of strong flowing curves. A path sweeps
around the lawn, terminating at the gazebo,
which is situated to act as a focal point. The
transformation of the top lawn into a
secret garden is completed by the addition of
a multistemmed birch that screens the
overlooking window.*

At this stage you can try anything, so why not see
how your designs would look? You can do this by
staging a sort of trial run, either starting from scratch or
reproducing one of your overlay designs. This often
works best as a two-person or family job—children will
love to help and it can be great fun getting the various
shapes pegged out. You will need some buckets full of
sand, stakes, poles, string and possibly a few trellis

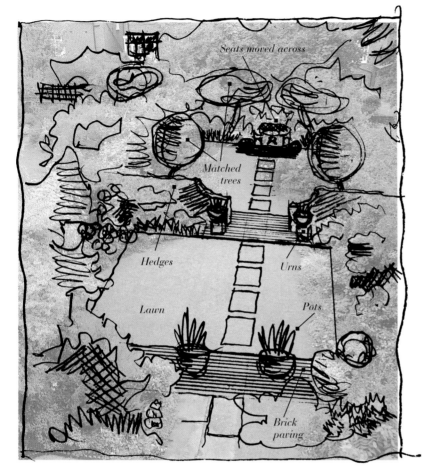

Seats moved across

Matched trees

Hedges

Urns

Lawn

Pots

Brick paving

Left *Formality brings a sense of control and stability. The neat apron of brick paving extends the terrace, and from here stepping stones cross the lawn before pausing at the hedges and classical urns. These provide a "tension point," partially hiding the second lawn and giving an air of mystery. The furniture has been centered at the end of the vista, and the matched pairs of pots, urns and trees add to the rhythm of the composition.*

panels. Go upstairs with your plan and start to direct the troops from your window. Curves can be marked out with a trickle of sand, which can easily be moved one way or another, trellises can be positioned to simulate a hedge or screen, while stakes can be driven in to indicate new trees. Free-form pools or island beds can be marked out with sand, while more architectural shapes can be marked with short poles and string. Pots

and furniture can easily be moved around, helping you to visualize new sight lines and focal points. Once you are happy with a particular scheme, leave everything in place, so that you can look at it over a few days or weeks. This will allow you to make adjustments before preparing a detailed plan.

detailed plans

Once you have really refined your ideas you can transfer them onto a detailed plan that is drawn to scale. Don't be intimidated: a scale drawing is simply an accurate representation of your garden in miniature, allowing you to plot every detail in proportion to the others and the site as a whole. Scales can confuse people who are not used to dealing with them; the easiest way to explain them is to say that your actual garden is at a scale of 1:1. A garden planned at 1:20 means the drawing is twenty times smaller, 1:50 means that it is fifty times smaller and so on. All of this means you can draw your garden in proportion, using all the measurements you gathered in the earlier stages of the planning process, on a manageable sheet of paper. Most average garden plots can be represented at scales of 1:18 or 1:36. Squared graph paper will be easiest to work on, each square representing a given distance on the ground. If you are working in a scale of 1:36, this means that 1 inch on the paper represents 1 yard on the ground. A drawing at 1:18 shows 2 inches for every 1 yard. Take your time in transferring the measurements from your rough plan to the scale drawing—a small change in figures at this stage can make a dramatic difference if carried through to the real garden.

First, create a scale survey drawing—an accurate representation of your garden as it is now—then make some photocopies and file the original away for safekeeping. The next step is to add the outlines of the garden as you want them to be. When preparing a design we always use tracing paper laid *over* the gridded survey drawing. The advantage of this technique is that you can prepare as many versions of your new garden design as you want, until you are completely happy with your new garden.

Remember to keep things simple and generous, with no awkward "pinch" points or very narrow borders next to the boundaries.

Below *In this garden of average size the main task was to provide a real feeling of space and movement, leading the eye away from the dominant boundaries. As one moves away from the house there is ample room for sitting and dining, with the area extending around two sides of the building to give access to both the lounge and kitchen areas. The main lawn and border shapes are bounded by areas of stone that merge with one another, bringing fluidity to the design.*

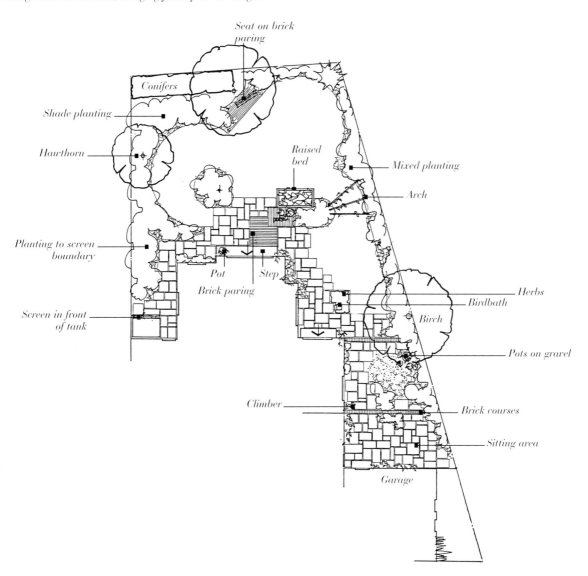

Seat on brick
paving

Conifers

Shade planting

Hawthorn

Raised
bed

Mixed planting

Arch

Planting to screen
boundary

Pot   Step

Herbs

Brick paving

Birdbath

Birch

Screen in front
of tank

Pots on gravel

Climber

Brick courses

Sitting area

Garage

The advantage of drawing your garden to scale is that you can see exactly how the layout fits together and the amount of paving slabs or turf you need. The first stage is the layout plan, which shows the "hard landscape" structure of the garden, including paving, walling, paths and the exact shape of lawns, borders and other features. We have already seen that areas close to the house should be architectural in character, and now you can accurately draw out a terrace, each slab or bricked area represented on the grid below. Here you can incorporate raised beds or a pool, built-in furniture or a barbecue. Paving patterns will look most comfortable if started from the corner of the building or other salient point, which will positively link it back to the architecture of the house. As you move away from the house those curves can come into play, but make them *positive* by using a pair of compasses and letting one radius flow into the next. Remember to keep things simple and generous, with no awkward "pinch points" or very narrow borders next to the boundaries. Mark in those screens, hedges and other dividers, as well as the major focal points, trees, steps and changes of level.

Once the layout plan is complete you can work out the planting on a separate sheet of tracing paper, placed over the former, and indicate just what plant goes where. Do your homework with regard to the soil type, sun and shade needed, and bear in mind the layering and color techniques that I explained earlier. Draw each plant at its adult size, using drifts and groups that will grow together to reduce maintenance. When drawing a plan, most people underestimate the size of plants, which leads to overcrowding, so it really is important to check just how big different species will eventually grow.

Opposite *The second part of the plan for your garden consists of a separate planting plan. Planting plans really are enormously helpful in allowing you to work out and visualize the finished garden, as they enable you to think of the planting almost in isolation, once the hard surfaces and structures have all been finalized. Just as planting forms another layer of the garden over the basic structure, so the planting should consist of different layers in itself. When building up the various layers, position them in relation to areas or views that may need screening or shelter, allocate positions for feature plants and work out your color schemes. You can see from my planting plan how the various groups and drifts work, the one overlapping the other to build up a pattern that reinforces the underlying design. One very important point is to draw the mature size of plants accurately to scale. A common mistake is to show plants too small, which in turn can mean that you overplant the garden.*

Paving patterns will look most comfortable if started from the corner of the building or other salient point, which will positively link it back to the architecture of the house.

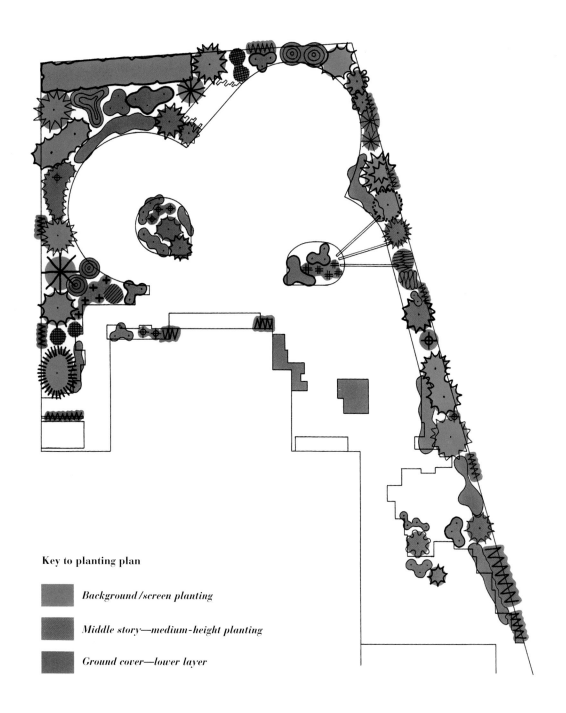

Key to planting plan

Background/screen planting

Middle story—medium-height planting

Ground cover—lower layer

Don't be intimidated: a scale drawing is simply an accurate representation of your garden in miniature, allowing you to plot every detail in proportion to the others and the site as a whole.

Opposite *The strict geometric lines of a garden such as this demand careful planning and attention to detail.*

implementing the plan

Now that you have created a detailed scale drawing on paper, it is time to transfer your design outside to your garden. This is not difficult and, again, it is good fun. In effect you are working in reverse from the design stage, and by measuring your drawing you can accurately transfer and position features in the garden. Remember that at a scale of 1:36, 1 inch on the drawing equals 1 yard in the garden. In other words, a terrace area measuring 4 inches x 4 inches on your scale drawing translates to 4 yards x 4 yards on the ground—easy! The best way to implement the design is to work *away* from the house, marking out and constructing the terrace or patio area first. Here you will almost certainly be working with rectangular shapes that use the building as their starting point. This area then provides the base for the rest of the design, which will flow away from it, and it will be easy enough to mark out the lines of borders that extend from the terrace.

Now comes the question of curves and how to swing these accurately. On your layout plan, if you used a pair of compasses as I suggested, you will have made a radius point that you will be able to see. Measure the position of this point from the layout plan, locating it by the distances from the house and boundary, and mark the position with a stake in the garden. Now you can swing a string line from the stake to mark the radius on the ground with a trail of sand. This line can be juggled if necessary, by adjusting the radius stake slightly. The curves of the garden will now start to link together and the various features and focal points can next be positioned in relation to these. If at this stage you want to make minor adjustments, then do so—no plan or design is cast in stone, and professionals often suggest easing a feature or line one way or another.

Once the design has been accurately pegged out you can do the same for the plants. If beds and borders are relatively small, it should be easy enough simply to lay these out by eye, but if the area is a large one, it may be better to use a grid system. This involves drawing a grid on the planting plan, say 2 inches square, that divides the bed into groups of plants. Now transfer this grid onto the ground by scaling up the measurements, marking out the lines with string or sand. It will now be straightforward to position the plants from your plan into the actual beds.

Opposite *When you come actually to lay the plants out in the borders it can be useful to work from a grid made up of 1- or 2-yard squares. This is particularly the case if you have a large border to plant, since it prevents much shuffling around of plants on the ground. Draw this grid on your planting plan initially and then transfer it, to scale, into the garden. Use poles and string to recreate the lines of the planting grid on the ground. Plants shown within a certain square can then be easily placed within a corresponding square on the ground.*

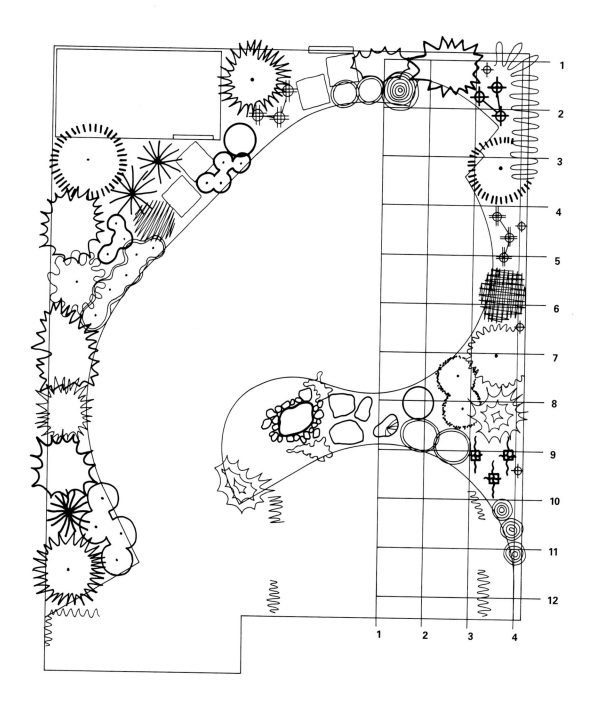

planning the work

Rome was not built in a day, and neither are most gardens. This means that you can take your time and develop the space as your funds or your busy lifestyle permit. In many ways it makes sound sense to work in phases, and the design normally breaks itself down into manageable areas. The one that is usually tackled first is the terrace or patio area. This is a major item and will probably take the lion's share of your overall budget. This is where the design is useful since it allows you to exactly estimate the amount of materials you will need for the job. From here the shapes of the borders can be cut out, and it will be easy enough to estimate the cost of plants from visits to competitive nurseries or garden centers.

Individual features, such as garden buildings, arches, arbors and pools, can be individually priced and phased into your overall plan. Some construction work can be done using labor-saving machinery, such as jackhammers, posthole diggers and garden tillers. Some of these machines may be easily managed by nonprofessionals, but some may not, so don't hesitate to get professional help if you need it.

A final option is to have the whole garden, or parts of it, built by professional landscape contractors. Choose these carefully, on recommendation if possible, and always ask them to quote competitively on the design you have prepared.

Opposite *It is easy to become confused about when to carry out the tasks needed to transfer your garden plan to the ground. This sample timeline might be used for a garden in the Pacific Northwest, or in similar areas of the USDA's hardiness zone 8. Contact your local nursery or cooperative extension office for help with developing an appropriate planting schedule for your area.*

Rome was not built in a day,
and neither are most gardens.

January	Start planning spring landscape projects
February	Plan vegetable gardens and order seeds Start landscape projects
March	Start planting new shrubs, trees and perennials Prepare new lawn areas Continue landscape projects
April	Plant shrubs, trees and perennials Seed new lawns Continue landscape projects
May	Finish spring planting of shrubs, trees and perennials Plant annuals Plant container-grown plants Plant aquatics
June	Plant shrubs and trees if able to irrigate
July	Continue planting trees and shrubs if able to irrigate Prepare new lawn areas for seeding Start planning new landscape projects
August	Seed new lawn areas Lay land drains if necessary Start new landscape projects
September	Carry out autumn planting of shrubs, trees and ground covers if hot weather is over Have all seeding done by the end of the month Continue landscape projects
October	Finish planting shrubs and trees Finish drainage work before rainy season starts Start planting bulbs
November	Prepare beds for next season; dig over beds and borders if necessary Finish planting bulbs
December	Start thinking about new plants for next year

case studies

Theory is a fine thing, but to really put to use those tricks of the trade, gardening rules and your sound common sense, it can help to see how they have been applied in real gardens by real people. I have chosen gardens in five very different situations, each of which has a wealth of ideas woven into particularly successful designs.

Right *This is a small urban garden that sloped up from the house. The space had been terraced but without any form of cohesion, with crude steps connecting the levels. Planting was virtually nonexistent, while high brick walls produced a feeling of claustrophobia.*

Opposite *By regrading the garden and cleverly dividing and punctuating space, the atmosphere of oppression and enclosure in this garden has been transformed into one of anticipation and adventure, with delights around every corner.*

walled garden

Transform a garden from walled-in corner to walk-in wonder.

Town gardens have their own special problems, often including high, oppressive walls, bad views and exhausted soil. This garden was no exception, and in addition it had a difficult change in level that divided the plot into two awkward areas.

The designer, Christopher Pickard, set out to tackle all of these problems by creating an integrated design, using a subtle blend of hard and soft landscape elements. A storage shed was needed in the garden, and this has been incorporated against the boundary wall at the far end. The doorway sets up the main axis of the new composition and is offset from the center line of the garden, providing a particularly comfortable visual division between left and right. Instead of retaining the existing arrangement of steps, the whole garden has been regraded so that the steps are both shallower and spaced at different intervals down the pathway. The latter is constructed from reclaimed stone slabs and pavers, the contrast of materials setting up an interesting, irregular rhythm. The weathered stone balls

add punctuation. The space is divided by a beautifully detailed screen, which doubles as an archway over the path. This has the effect of bringing the eye down into the garden and diminishing the impact of the high surrounding walls. Notice how the wooden balls on top of the screen echo those on the ground, a particularly subtle touch. By forming two separate garden rooms, the screen also creates a delicious feeling of anticipation, mystery and surprise. Just before you pass under the arch you catch a glimpse of the seat to the right. This cross axis lends visual width to the garden.

As this is essentially an architectural garden, planting is important to soften the crisp outlines. A strong framework of shrubs, including evergreens for winter interest, is tempered with hardy perennials, which introduce delicacy and color. Such a garden will not only look good throughout the year but will require relatively little maintenance.

Right The secret of this design is a subtle manipulation of space division, with hard and soft landscape features that break the view across the garden, dividing it into separate rooms. The trellis frames are highly detailed, and these are in direct contrast to the planting, which softens their outline, providing color and interest throughout the year. The planting is carried out with a plantsman's eye, producing some excellent combinations of shape, pattern and texture.

Above *In a walled garden, climbers are essential for breaking the line of such hard boundaries and take planting boldly into the third dimension. In a sheltered environment fragrance comes into its own, and roses are particularly valuable in this respect.*
Right *It is remarkable that even the smallest of spaces can be effectively subdivided to create different areas. Such an approach does of course make the overall garden feel larger. This comfortable bench, set to one side on a cross axis, provides a delightfully secluded corner.*

small country garden

Garden design begins at home.

Above This was my garden. We started off with pretty much nothing at all apart from a wasteland of builder's rubble. The soil was poor and very stony so the first job was to dig in as much organic matter as possible, simply to give plants any chance at all.

Opposite The sight and sound of the water, the sense of space created by the broad steps, and the contrast between heavy planting and sharp architectural lines combine to make a striking garden that changes character with the seasons.

This is my own garden, and as such it has to work hard for a living. It is virtually square, measuring about half an acre, with a drop of 6½ feet from top to bottom. Originally it was completely derelict, with a steep and oppressive bank immediately outside the back door. The house and adjoining barn are built from a combination of brick and stone, dating from about 1650, and this set the theme for the materials used in the landscaping. Being a contemporary designer, I wanted to create a garden that would reflect my professional style, while requiring minimal maintenance since I am often away from home.

I have a great love of water, and I also wanted to experiment with planting that would serve both to attract wildlife and to set up divisions within the composition. We provided ample room for sitting and dining, using both simulated stone and brick paving to

provide a visual link with the building. The slope was completely reworked into a series of broad terraces that work their way up through the garden. Steps are broad and generous, their outlines softened by planting. The garden is given visual width by parallel bands of water, hedging, planting and lawn. This feeling of width is increased by wide gravel paths that are set to each side, rather than up the middle; their outlines are cushioned by grasses and herbs that are fragrant, practical and handsome. The restful sounds of water emanate from the main pool, some 13 yards long, which drops over a fall and into a stream, heavily planted with aquatic species that attract birds and other wildlife.

It is hard to believe that there are no curves at all in this garden as the planting provides a simple but subtle backdrop. I have made a conscious decision to use a high proportion of herbaceous plants that die down in winter, to emphasize the hard landscape structure that is complemented by shimmering sheets of water.

Above I love features tucked away in unexpected places. This grotesque mask, which I added after the garden was completed, sits beneath the waterfall that drops from the long pool into the stream below. He forms a focal point for the view from the kitchen windows—in summer water dances over his features and in winter he is encrusted with frost and ice. All of this proves the point that sometimes you just have to wait for the right ornament or "found object" to come along.

Right *Pots are wonderful for injecting a dash of color and interest in a specific area. They should be as big as reasonably possible to keep plants happy. This geranium seeded itself and I've kept it ever since. The seat in the background is set at the end of a long pool, in a sunny location.*

Above *This a view looking across the long pool planted with yellow iris and all kinds of aquatics. Fish, dragonflies and wildlife abound. At the back of the pool is a bed planted with just a single species of white grass (Phalaris 'Feesey's Form'), which makes a powerful statement in both summer and winter.*

Above right *This rambling rose cascading over a fence is called 'Goldfinch' and is very fragrant. The flowering season is relatively short, only a month or so, but for that time it is absolute perfection.*

Right *This is one of my favorite views of the garden—broad, easy steps climbing the slope. The gravel path is 6½ft wide and this allows ample room for plants to tumble over the sides. The metal guinea fowl come from South Africa, and the pithoi jars from Crete. These kinds of treasures help to bring a garden to life, awakening memories of places you have visited.*

suburban garden

Asymmetrical design and low-maintenance planting create a suburban oasis of calm and tranquility.

Suburban gardens outnumber all others, and unfortunately, this one was both small and unpromising. As is typical of other gardens of its type, it has poor views (of neighboring houses and garages) and dominant brick walls. In addition, there was little worthwhile in the way of planting. The owner wanted a low-maintenance solution. The lawn was to be eliminated and a small water feature provided.

Barbara Hunt, the designer, has a wonderful eye for detail and created a delightful, asymmetrical composition that fulfills the brief perfectly. There is a delicate balance between hard and soft landscape elements, the main part of the garden being accessed by a staggered path that helps to increase the visual width of the plot. The terraced area to the left is a subtle combination of neat, precast paving slabs separated by courses of brick;

Left *It is hard to believe that this was once such a disappointing area! The introduction of a water feature and several other ingenious focal points draws attention away from the unattractive surroundings and focuses the eye on the beauty of the garden itself. Planting around the boundaries of the garden has worked wonders, disguising those features that could easily cause despair—you would hardly believe that this leafy arbor softens and hides the adjoining garage.*

Above *The blank brick wall is brought alive by this elegant water feature, which is in turn linked to the wider garden with sculptural planting.*

Opposite *In this high-level view you can see how the ground plan works, with paved bands pushing out into the gravel floor. Planting completely masks the garden outline, neutralizing the rectangular shape.*

these lead the eye out to the neat gravel floor, which is softened and surrounded by planting. Overhead, beams play host to climbers such as vines and clematis, which provide dappled shade, as well as breaking the dominant line of the next-door garage. On the opposite side of the garden a striking contemporary water feature provides the main focal point of the design. Water slides from a V-shaped trough onto two blocks of slate, cleverly set in juxtaposition to one another, before being recycled via an underground pump. This focal point is just one of the features cleverly introduced by Barbara Hunt. Where she has not been able to hide unattractive features of the garden, she has introduced other elements to draw attention away from them. So while she is never going to be able to knock down adjoining houses or immediately cover a huge brick wall with attractive climbers, she is able to introduce focal points that draw attention to the interior of the garden, away from the boundaries. The problem of ugly views is solved because the visitors have enough to occupy them within the boundaries of the garden, so there is no need to look outside.

A good garden has the ability to turn its back on uncompromising surroundings, creating its own world than can be completely self-contained. The challenge is in taking the original framework and reclothing it so that it takes on an altogether different persona.

roof terrace

Taming the space creates a garden on top of the world.

Gardening high above the street brings its own problems of difficult access, high winds, bright light and burning sun. Having said that, if you can meet the challenge of turning all these drawbacks into positive advantages, you can have a garden on top of the world, with stunning views that are as good at night as they are during the day. When that view is of the city of New York, with its dazzling array of skyscrapers and traffic far below, you have the potential for something very special indeed.

The first problem to overcome with any roof garden is the question of weight, and it is vitally important to have the load-bearing potential checked by a professional architect or building engineer and be guided by any provisos they may stipulate. Irrigation should also be taken into account at the planning stage and can easily be incorporated during construction, saving an enormous amount of work later on.

The main planting areas are positioned around the edges of the rooftop. This is sensible since the strongest

part of any roof is around the perimeter, where the ceiling supports adjoin the outside walls. Even lightweight composts and building materials are heavy, particularly when wet—so try to use containers made of modern materials such as fiberglass, which will keep the weight down. Planting mostly around the edges also leaves the main part of the garden open for sitting, dining and entertaining.

Since it is impossible to dig down, beds are raised, which also offers the opportunity for plants to cascade over the edges, softening the outlines and providing partial shelter. The planting in this garden is particularly subtle, with drought-tolerant species setting up a fascinating dialogue of shape, size and texture. Between the beds, plate glass panels allow tantalizing glimpses of the city below.

With such bright light, color is an important aspect of this garden; the thin terra-cotta tiles are an ideal foil for the off-white walls. Large areas of pure white should always be avoided, as the glare can be intolerable.

Above and left *The secret to this garden is subtle containment, with planting softening the look of the perimeter walls and glass screens. As foliage is of variable height and density it allows views of the city beyond. What is particularly attractive is the variety of plant material, ranging from fastigiate conifers that echo the downtown skyline to low-growing ground covers and grasses. Growing conditions may be difficult up here, but the effort is more than worth it.*

Above *What I really like about this garden is the space—there is a huge amount of room for all kinds of outdoor activities. Once the force of the wind is broken with screens and plantings, the temperatures are benign, allowing a range of plant material that would be impossible to grow in the colder climate outside the city. The warm-colored terra-cotta tiles are just right to tone down the effect of strong sunlight, and the laying pattern leads your eye down to the tree that acts as a wonderful and unexpected focal point so high above ground level.*

small urban garden

Dramatic planting and decking transform a small, dark garden into an attractive outside room.

Above *Small was certainly not beautiful in this instance, with awkward access, oppressive boundaries and little in the way of positive planting. On the other hand, any situation has potential, and this clean slate of a garden was sheltered, secluded and, when completed, easy to maintain.*

There is often far too much doom and gloom in people's attitudes about urban gardens, even if they *are* small, dark and seemingly difficult to deal with. Like so many others that are deep in the heart of a city, the access for this garden was awkward, down impossibly steep and dangerous steps. The boundaries were oppressive, hemming the space in, while the main floor area was simply rubble and a few sparse shrubs. The advantages, however, were considerable in that the surrounding trees screened adjoining properties, which in turn provided shelter and a mild microclimate. In this kind of situation you have a completely clean slate to work with. The mission here was to create an outside room in the fullest sense.

The first job was to resolve the problem of access. The old steps were demolished, making way for new

Right *One of the best ways to see the workings of a garden is from above, where everything is visible at a glance. From this level the structure is clearly apparent, as are the various elements and the ways they relate to one another. As you make your way down the steps the sight lines change, the new planting offers definition and enclosure, and the whole garden takes on the composition of an outdoor room.*

stairs that, instead of descending in a straight line, drop down in two leisurely flights, turned at right angles to one another.

In many small urban gardens, a lawn is difficult, if not out of the question, since the shady conditions and heavy wear-and-tear would quickly reduce any grass to a quagmire. Instead, you should think of choosing a simple but tough surface—in this case brick paving— that also provides a visual link with the building.

The old panel fences, which were stark and oppressive, have been replaced by bamboo, which is far less obtrusive, providing an excellent foil for planting. This needs a good deal of thought, since in a small area

large shrubs can quickly outgrow the available space. Careful research should be undertaken before planting a small space, taking care to find out the size and spread that mature plants will eventually reach. The choice of plants in this garden is particularly clever—a number of pale, small-leaved species that not only lighten the area but break the line of the boundaries with their shimmering silhouettes. Remember that large-leaved plants would do just the opposite, making the boundaries seem closer than they really are. As a final delicate touch, woven furniture has been added to blend with the fencing and garden as a whole.

Opposite *In an intimate space the planting area is restricted. Because of this you should exercise control over the plants you choose and the way you use them. Species like New Zealand flax offer a strong architectural outline, but they also have the potential to outgrow the available space. Don't be afraid to replace or remove such plants after a while—you have to remember who is boss in such a small garden!*

Below *In a limited space you need to organize things carefully. Too much paving and there is little room for anything else. Here, there is a delicate and well-worked balance between the two elements.*

Right *Gardens are a place for leisure and horticulture. This comfortable chair, entwined by trailing nasturtiums in bloom, sums up an easygoing but successful mix of hard and soft landscape materials.*

address book

Vermont Brick
Box 330
Highgate Center, VT 05459
Tel: (802) 868-5354 for catalog
Fax: (802) 868-5438

*Bricks for use in paths, paving
and architecture*

Garden Structures

Oak Leaf Conservatories
876 Davis Drive
Atlanta, GA 30327
Tel: (800) 360-6283 for catalog
Fax: (404) 250-6283

Glass enclosures

Summerwood Products
733 Progress Avenue
Toronto, Ontario
Canada M1H 2W7
Tel: (800) 663-5042
Fax: (416) 431-2454
E-mail: info@summerwood.com
Web site: www.summerwood.com

*Gazebos, garden sheds, pool
cabanas*

Vixen Hill Gazebos
Dept GD-0 Main Street
Elverson, PA 19520
Tel: (800) 423-2766 for catalog
Fax: (610) 286-2099
E-mail: vixenhill@vixenhill.com
Web site: www.vixenhill.com

*Modular cedar gazebos and
screened garden houses*

Walpole Woodworkers
767 East Street
Walpole, MA 02081
Tel: (800) 343-6948 for catalog
Fax: (508) 668-7301

*Hand-crafted cedar arches,
arbors, trellises, fences, lantern
posts and garden furniture*

**American Horticultural
Society**
7931 East Boulevard Drive
Alexandria, VA 22308
Tel: (703) 768-5700
Fax: (703) 768-8700
Web site: www.ahs.org

American Rose Society
P.O. Box 30,000
Shreveport, LA 71130-0030
Tel: (318) 938-5402
Fax: (318) 938-5405
E-mail: ars@ars-hq.org
Web site: www.ars.org

**American Society of
Landscape Architects**
636 Eye Street, NW
Washington, D.C. 20001-3736
Tel: (202) 898-2444
Fax: (202) 898-1155
E-mail: scahill@asla.org
Web site: www.asla.org

Garden Club of America
14 East 60th Street
New York, NY 10022
Tel: (212) 753-8287
Fax: (212) 753-0134
E-mail: info@gcamerica.org
Web site: www.gcamerica.org

Decking

**Mendocino Specialty
Lumber Company**
P.O. Box 519
Hydesville, CA 95547
Tel: (707) 726-0339
Fax: (707) 726-0319
E-mail: wood@oldgrowth.com
Web site: www.oldgrowth.com

*Reclaimed wood from old-
growth redwood trees harvested
before 1930*

Screens and Dividers

Sycamore Creek
P.O. Box 16
Ancram, NY 12502
Tel: (518) 398-6393
Fax: (518) 398-7697
E-mail:
sycamorecreek@taconic.net
Web site:
www.sycamorecreek.com

Copper trellises and arbors

Trellis Structures
P.O. Box 380
Beverly, MA 01915
Tel: (978) 921-1235 for catalog
Fax: (978) 232-1151
E-mail:
pcornell@trellisstructures.com
Web site:
www.trellisstructures.com

Cedar trellises and arbors

Natural Stone, Brick and Precast Paving

ASN Natural Stone
200 Kansas Street, Suite 209
San Francisco, CA 94103
Tel: (415) 626-2616 or
(800) 827-8663
Fax: (415) 626-3578
E-mail: asnstone@pacbell.net
Web site: www.asnstone.com

*Imported natural stone for
indoor and outdoor uses*

Dixie Cut Stone & Marble
6128 Dixie Highway
Bridgeport, MI 48722
Tel: (800) 968-8282
Fax: (517) 777-9700
E-mail: limestone@dixiestone.com
Web site: www.dixiestone.com

*Architectural landscaping stone,
limestone, marble and other
natural stones*

Rhodes Masonry, Inc.
2011 East Olive Street
Seattle, WA 98122
Tel: (206) 726-0437
Fax: (206) 709-3004 or 709-3003
E-mail: info@rhodesmasonry.com
Web site:
www.rhodesmasonry.com

*Architectural stone, brick and
precast paving*

Irrigation Systems

Affordable Premier Sprinklers, Inc.
13527 Leedwick Drive
Houston, TX 77041
Tel: (713) 937-7347
Fax: (713) 937-9967
E-mail:
steve@affordablesprinklers.com
Web site:
www.affordablesprinklers.com

Irrigation systems for lawns

International Irrigation Systems, Inc.
1755 Factory Outlet Boulevard
Box 163
Niagara Falls, NY 14304-0163
Tel: (905) 688-4090
Fax: (905) 688-4093
E-mail: support@irrigro.com
Web site: www.irrigro.com

Drip irrigation systems

Garden Lighting

Escort Lighting
51 North Elm Street
Wernersville, PA 19565
Tel: (800) 856-7948 for brochure
Fax: (610) 670-5170

Solid copper garden lighting

Garden Furniture, Containers and Accessories

Brown Jordan International
9860 Gidley Street
El Monte, CA 91731
Tel: (800) 743-4252
Fax: (626) 575-0126

Contemporary and traditional lounge furniture

The Grass Roots Garden
313 Spring Street
New York, NY 10012
Tel: (212) 226-2662
Fax: (212) 274-1887

Wide range of pots, containers and supplies for the garden

Kinsman Company
River Road
Point Pleasant, PA 18950-0357
Tel: (800) 396-1251 for catalog
Web site:
www.kinsmangarden.com

Hand-welded steel planters, containers and hanging baskets

Mecox Gardens
257 County Road 39A
Southampton, NY 11968
Tel: (516) 287-5015
Fax: (516) 287-5018
E-mail: wmhmecox@aol.com
Web site:
www.mecoxgardens.com or
www.bestselections.com

Home and garden furniture and accessories

Smith & Hawken
2 Arbor Lane, Box 6900
Florence, KY 41022-6900
Tel: (800) 776-3336
Fax: (606) 727-1166
Web site:
www.smithandhawken.com

Garden furniture, tools and supplies

Treillage
418 East 75th Street
New York, NY 10021
Tel: (212) 535-2288
Fax: (212) 517-6589

Antiques and reproduction ornaments, containers and fixtures for the garden

Garden Supplies

American Soil Products
2222 Third Street
Berkeley, CA 94710
Tel: (510) 540-8011
Fax: (510) 540-8066
Web site: www.americansoil.com

Soils and mulches, plus stone slabs, boulders, cobbles and other stone products

Gardener's Supply Company
128 Intervale Road
Burlington, VA 05401
Tel: (800) 863-1700 for catalog
Fax: (800) 876-5520
Web site: www.gardeners.com

Tools, irrigation equipment, fertilizers and other garden supplies

Statuary

Elegant Accents West Inc.
604 McClary Avenue
Oakland, CA 94621
Tel: (510) 568-6255 for catalog
Fax: (510) 568-6360
E-mail: elegant@pacbell.net
Web site:
www.gardendiscovery.com

Stone and bamboo Japanese garden ornaments

Haddonstone
201 Heller Place
Interstate Business Park
Bellmawr, NJ 08031
Tel: (856) 931-7011 for catalog
Fax: (856) 931-0040

Classical and Italianate landscape ornaments and architectural cast stonework

Planting

W. Atlee Burpee & Co.
Warminister, PA 18974
Tel: (800) 888-1447 for catalog
Fax: (800) 487-5530
Web site: www.burpee.com

Plants, bulbs and seeds, including heirloom varieties

Etera
14113 River Bend Road
Mount Vernon, WA 98273
Tel: (800) 753-8372
Fax: (360) 424-8537
E-mail: info@etera.com
Web site: www.etera.com

Perennials

Henry Field's Seed & Nursery Co.
415 North Burnett
Shenandoah, IA 51602
Tel: (800) 798-7842 or
(605) 665-4491 for catalog
Fax: (605) 665-2601
Web site: www.henryfields.com
or www.myseasons.com

Seeds and plants; fruit, nut and shade trees

Johnny's Selected Seeds
Foss Hill Road
Albion, ME 04910
Tel: (207) 437-4301
Fax: (800) 437-4290
E-mail:
homegarden@johnnyseeds.com
or johnnys@johnnyseeds.com
Web site: www.johnnyseeds.com

Organic flower, vegetable and herb seeds

Miller Nurseries
5060 West Lake Road
Canandaigua, NY 14424
Tel: (800) 836-9630
Fax: (716) 396-2154

Fruit and nut trees, berries and flowers

Shepherd's Garden Seeds
30 Irene Street
Torrington, CT 06790-6658
Tel: (860) 482-3638
Fax: (860) 482-0532
E-mail:
custsrv@shepherdseeds.com
Web site:
www.shepherdseeds.com

Plants, seeds and bulbs

index

First published in 2000 by
Conran Octopus Limited
a part of Octopus Publishing Group
2–4 Heron Quays
London E14 4JP

www.conran-octopus.co.uk

Text copyright © David Stevens 2000
Design and layout copyright © Conran Octopus 2000

SOMA Books is an imprint of Bay Books & Tapes,
555 De Haro St., No. 220, San Francisco, CA 94107.

For the Conran Octopus edition:
Commissioning Editor: Stuart Cooper
Senior Editor: Helen Woodhall
Copy Editor: Helena Attlee
Editorial Assistant: Alexandra Kent

Creative Director: Leslie Harrington
Designer: Lucy Gowans
Picture Researcher: Mel Watson
Production Controller: Suzanne Sharpless

For the SOMA edition:
Copy Editor: Karen O'Donnell Stein
Proofreader: Ken DellaPenta
Production: Jeff Brandenburg

Library of Congress Cataloging-in-Publication Data

Stevens, David, 1943-
    SOMA Basics—Garden Design/ David Stevens
    —North American ed.
    p.cm.—(SOMA Basics)
    Rev. ed. of: Conran Octopus contemporary garden design.
    2000.
    ISBN 1-57959-061-6 (pbk.)
    1. Gardens—Design. I. Title: Garden design. II. Stevens,
David, 1943–Conran Octopus contemporary garden design. III.
Title. IV. Series.

    SB473 .S84283 2000
    712'.6—dc21
    00-027990

Printed in China
10 9 8 7 6 5 4 3 2 1
Distributed by Publishers Group West

Author's acknowledgments

A finished book is only the tip of an iceberg of planning and hard work involving far more people than the author! Special thanks to my editor, Helen Woodhall, my secretary, Angela Bambridge, Nicola Stocken-Thomas, who photographed my garden and Jack Sexton who built it.

Publisher's acknowledgments

The publisher would like to thank the following photographers and agencies for their kind permission to reproduce the photographs in this book:
2 Simon Kenny/Belle Magazine/Designers: Marsh & Cashman, Australia; **4–5** Andrea Jones/Garden Exposures; **7** John Edward Linden/Arcaid/Architect: Mark Guard; **9** Marianne Majerus/Designer: Will Giles, Norwich; **10–11** Andrea Jones/Garden Exposures; **13** Mark Bolton/The Garden Picture Library; **14** *left* Steven Wooster; **14–15** Ursel Borstell; **15** Andrea Jones courtesy Boxtree designed by Paul Thompson & Ann-Marie Powell; **17** Jeremy Cockayne/Arcaid/Architect: Pierre d'Avoine; **21** Bart van Leuven/Landscape Architects: Pieter Ingelaere & Dominique Eeman, Belgium; **22–23** Thompson & Morgan, Suffolk; Mr Fothergill's Seeds, Suffolk; Town & Country Paving Ltd, West Sussex; Russell & Chapple Ltd, London; Indian Ocean Trading Company, London; **23** Michael Paul/Designer: Anthony Paul; **24** *above* J C Mayer–G Le Scanff/Designer: Eric Ossart & Arnaud Maurieres, Jardin des Fournials, France; **24** *below* Jerry Harpur/Designer: Leslie Walford, Sydney; **25** Bart van Leuven/Landscape Architect: Peter Cattoir, Belgium; **27** Jerry Harpur/Dr Lyons, CA, USA; **28–29** S & O Mathews, R.H.S. Garden, Wisley; **30** Liz Eddison/Designers: Bunny Guinness & Peter Eustace/Chelsea Flower Show 1999, Wyevale Garden Centres; **34** *left* Howard Rice/The Garden Picture Library/Dorset College, Dorchester; **34** *right* Earl Carter/ Architect: Andrew Parr, SJB Interior Design, South Melbourne, Australia; **35** Jerry Harpur/Designer: Keith Corlett, New York; **36** Nicola Stocken Tomkins/ Designers: Ann & John Bracey; **37** Arcaid/Geoff Lung/Belle Magazine/Architect: Luigi Rosselli, Design Trilogy, Sydney, Australia; **38** *above* Liz Eddison/Designer: Gavin Landscaping/Chelsea Flower Show 1996; **38** *below* Derek St Romaine/Chelsea Flower Show 1999/Christie's Sculpture Garden/Designer: George Carter; **39** *left* Nicola Stocken Tomkins; **39** *above right* Steven Wooster; **39** *below right* Liz Eddison/Designer: Claire Whitehouse/Chelsea Flower Show 1999/Action for Blind People; **40** *left* Ron Sutherland/The Garden Picture Library/Designer: Anthony Paul; **40** *right* Liz Eddison/Designer: James Alexander-Sinclair/Chelsea Flower Show 1999/The Express Garden; **41** *left* Andrew Lawson; **41** *right* Bart van Leuven/ Landscape Architect: Paul Beyl, Belgium; **42** J S Sira/The Garden Picture Library; **43** Jerry Harpur/Designer: Robert Broekema, Amsterdam; **44** Ursel Borstell; **45** Spike Powell/Robert Harding Syndication/Inspirations Magazine; **46** *left* Leigh Clapp/The Mosaic Garden, Melbourne; **46** *right* Liz Eddison; **47** *left* C Simon-Sykes/Camera Press; **47** *right* Liz Eddison; **49** Gil Hanly/Architect: Ron Sang/Landscaping:Ted Smyth; **50** Sunniva Harte/The Garden Picture Library; **51** *above* Marianne Majerus/Designer: Mary Payne, Somerset; **51** *below* Hugh Palmer/Designer: Catriona Boyle; **52** *above* John Glover; **52** *center* John Glover/Designer: Susy Smith; **52** *below* Lorraine Pullin/The Garden Picture Library; **53** Andrea Jones courtesy Boxtree designed by Paul Thompson & Ann-Marie Powell; **54–55** Liz Eddison/Chelsea Flower Show 1996; **56–57** Clive Nichols, The Nichols Garden, Reading; **58–59** John Miller/The Garden Picture Library; **65** Jan Baldwin/Homes and Gardens/Robert Harding Syndication; **70–71** Nicola Stocken Tomkins; **72** Christopher Pickard; **73–75** Jerry Harpur/Designer: Christopher Pickard, Eccleshall, Staffs; **76** David Stevens; **77–79** Nicola Stocken Tomkins/Designer: David Stevens, Thornton, Bucks; **80** Barbara Hunt; **81–83** John Glover/Designer: Barbara Hunt, Staines, Middlesex/Owners: Mr & Mrs W. Sewell; **84** Jeff Mendoza; **85–87** Jerry Harpur/Garden Designer: Jeff Mendoza, J. Mendoza Gardens, 18 West 27th Street, New York, NY 10001, USA; **88–91** Andrea Jones courtesy Boxtree designed by Paul Thompson & Ann-Marie Powell.

We apologize in advance for any unintentional omission and would be pleased to insert the appropriate acknowledgment in any subsequent edition.

Thanks to Sarah Decker of Four Dimensions Landscape Development, 4121 Culver Street, Oakland, CA 94619; John Stone of Teufel Commercial Landscape, 12345 NW Barnes Road, Portland, OR 97229; and Michael Bronkala of Gardenstone Design, 6206 45th Avenue NE, Seattle, WA 98115.